Making Multiplication Easy

STRATEGIES FOR MASTERING THE TABLES THROUGH 10

by Meish Goldish

- x For Children of all Learning Styles and Strengths
- x Games, Songs, and Stories
- x Poems, Puzzles, Reproducibles, and More

SCHOLASTIC
PROFESSIONAL BOOKS

New York · Toronto · London · Auckland · Sydney

X X X X X X X X X X X X X X X X X X X X X X X X X X X

I am deeply indebted to two outstanding teachers, Roberta Annunziata and Judy O'Gorman, for their creative input in this book. They shared with me a vast array of clever and innovative techniques for teaching multiplication to children. Without their expert help, this book could not have been written. **M.G.**

Designed by Graphic Masters
Cover design by Anna V. Walker
Cover photograph by Jeff Heiges
Illustrated by Gaye Noble-Fete

ISBN 0-590-49140-7

Table of Contents

X Introduction

Multiplication may be a science, but *teaching* multiplication is an art. Traditionally, it's been taught by having students memorize flashcards. While that method works for some children, it does not work for all children. Even those who succeed in rote drills often do not fully understand what they're doing because they are not taught the practical applications of multiplication. In order for multiplication to have meaning, children must see its relevance. They need to recognize how the process can help them solve their own everyday problems.

Teaching multiplication is an art for another reason too: Not all children learn the same way. Some are visual learners; what they *see* is what they get. Others are auditory learners; what

they *hear* is what they get. And still others are kinesthetic learners; what they *handle* is what they get.

Making Multiplication Easy shows you how to make multiplication relevant in the lives of your students and provides you with effective teaching methods for every type of learner. It offers a variety of games, puzzles, songs, poems, and reproducible patterns to help teach the multiples of 1 through 10.

Throughout the book, you'll find the 🏠 icon next to certain activities. This icon indicates activities that students are encouraged to take home and share with their parents to reinforce classroom learning.

Now on with *Making Multiplication Easy*, which will enable you to make learning multiplication fun, practical, and painless.

X Easing Your Way into Multiplication

Children love shortcuts. Why walk around the puddle when you can zip right through it instead? By all accounts then, multiplication should be a welcome technique to children. After all, what is multiplication except a shortcut for addition?

Yet despite its attractions, many students remain intimidated by multiplication. Perhaps it's the length of the word.

Maybe it's that strange new symbol: X.

Whatever the reason, you may wish to ease your kids into multiplication without even using its name at first. How?

Clap If You Love the "M" Word

Start with this simple game: Ask students to count the times you clap your hands. Then clap three times. Kids will readily tell you the number: 3.

Now have kids listen again: "Clap—clap—clap (PAUSE), clap—clap—clap." Kids will say the number: 6.

On the board, write: $3 + 3 = 6$.

Now have the class listen one more time. Warn them that this time, however, there will be many more groups of three. Then begin:

"Clap—clap—clap (PAUSE), clap—clap—clap (PAUSE), clap—clap—clap (PAUSE), clap—clap—clap (PAUSE), clap—clap—clap (PAUSE), clap—clap—clap."

"How many claps in all?" 18.

"How many *groups of three?*" See who can tell you 6.

On the board, write:

$3 + 3 + 3 + 3 + 3 + 3 = 18$

6 groups of $3 = 18$

Now ask a volunteer to leave the classroom. While the child is out, have the class agree on a different clapping pattern. For example: "This time, let's clap in groups of five, and let's do four groups."

When the volunteer returns, have the class clap its pattern. The volunteer will listen and then write on the board the arithmetic statement that expresses the pattern:

$5 + 5 + 5 + 5 = 20$

4 groups of $5 = 20$

Play the game as many times as you like. Your class may not realize it, but they're clapping their way to multiplication!

Star Count

A game of Star Count is a stellar way to introduce multiplication too. Roll a pair of dice. Announce the number on one die and then draw that many circles on the chalkboard. Suppose you rolled a 4.

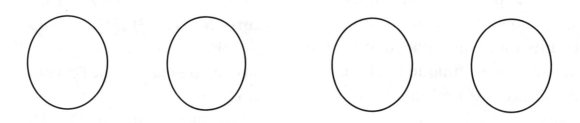

Now announce the number on the other die and draw that many stars inside each circle. Suppose you rolled a 2.

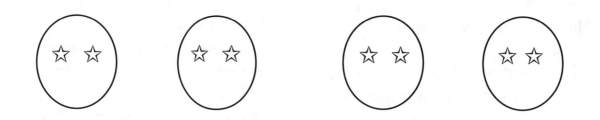

Ask students:

"How many stars are in each circle?"
"How many circles are there?"
"How many stars are there in all?"

On the board, write:

2 + 2 + 2 + 2 = 8

4 groups of 2 = 8

Choose a volunteer to try to beat you by getting a higher total of stars. The volunteer rolls the dice and draws his picture according to the numbers. The class counts the stars to see who wins.

The winner then writes the arithmetic statement that expresses his pattern.

Invite more students to play Star Count. See who ends up with the most stars. Can anyone guess the highest number of stars a player can get in the game? (36)

Row, Row, Row Your Disks

Still another way to approach multiplication is by arranging small plastic disks (or any other manipulative) in rows. For example:

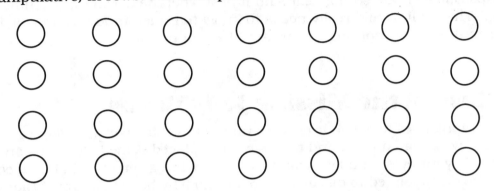

Ask the children to gather round. Invite them to touch the disks as they count how many are in each row.

"How many disks in every row?"
"How many rows?"
"How many disks in all?"

On the board, write:

4 disks in every row
7 rows in all
4 + 4 + 4 + 4 + 4 + 4 + 4 = 28
7 groups of 4 = 28

Some student is bound to ask, "Why do you say there are seven rows? I see four rows." Eureka! The disks can be viewed two different ways.

On the board, write:

7 disks in every row
4 rows in all
7 + 7 + 7 + 7 = 28
4 groups of 7 = 28

In a subtle and fun way, your students just discovered that 4 × 7 is the same as 7 × 4.

Multiplying by 0

Perhaps Shakespeare's King Lear said it best when he declared, "Nothing will come of nothing." That's all a child really needs to know to understand multiplying by zero: Any number multiplied by nothing will always give you nothing.

The Case of the Missing Jelly Beans

Use manipulatives to get your class to understand this concept. Ask your students to close their eyes. Wait a little, and then say, "I've placed some jelly beans on each of your desks. Open your eyes, and let's count how many I've given out in all." Of course, your kids will be disappointed to discover there are no jelly beans on any of the desks.

Ask students:

"How many jelly beans are on each desk?" (None.)

"How many desks do we have in class?" (Say, for example, there are 28.)

"So how many jelly beans do we have in all?" (None.)

On the chalkboard, write:

0	**×**	**28**	**=**	**0**
beans on each desk	×	desks	=	beans in all
0	**×**	**28**	**=**	**0**

Have students copy the statement 0 × 28 = 0 on their papers. Then tell them to draw a sad face inside each of the 0's. This little artwork will help them remember that nothing will come of nothing.

 × **28** =

Now say, "Suppose our room had fifty desks. If each desk had no jelly beans on it, would there still be no jelly beans altogether? What about one hundred desks?" Make the point that *any* number, when multiplied by zero, will give you zero. 14 gazillion times zero will still give you zero.

Read Those Signs Carefully!

In discovering that nothing will come of nothing, kids shouldn't develop the notion that any math statement involving a zero automatically yields an answer of zero. Multiplication does, but addition and subtraction, of course, do not.

$$7 \times 0 = 0 \quad \text{but} \quad 7 - 0 = 7$$

$$0 \times 7 = 0 \quad \text{but} \quad 0 + 7 = 7$$

This last exercise will remind your students to read those signs carefully! Now you may want to give each student a handful of jelly beans to restore their faith in your goodwill!

Super Challenge

Pose this brainteaser to your class:

"If you multiplied all the numbers on a telephone dial together ($1 \times 2 \times 3 \times 4$...and so on), what would the total be?"

The catch to this "phone-y" puzzler is that no actual calculation is required. Since the last number on the dial is 0, the final product will be 0!

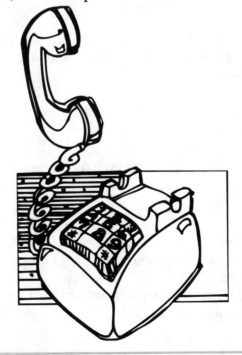

Multiplying by 1

Children may not realize it, but they've been multiplying by one ever since they heard their first once-upon-a-time story.

"Once upon a time there were three bears." How many bears are there? Three!

"Once upon a time there were seven dwarfs." How many dwarfs were there? Seven!

"Once upon a time there was a girl named Cinderella." How many Cinderellas were there? One!

"Once upon a time" means that everyone in the story existed just *once*—not twice, or four times, or ten times. Were the three bears really six bears? No, they were *three* bears who lived *once* upon a time. Or, to state it mathematically:

1 ✕ **3** bears **=** **3** bears

Nuts to You!

On the board, draw a peanut shell with two peanuts inside. Ask the class how many shells they see. Then ask how many peanuts are in the shell.

Write: **1** shell ✕ **2** peanuts **=** **2** peanuts in all

1 ✕ **2** **=** **2**

Continue by drawing a shamrock with four leaves, a hand with five fingers, a guitar with six strings, a calendar week with seven days, an octopus with eight arms, and a candlestick holder with nine candles.

For each drawing, ask "How many?" Invite a volunteer to write the math statement that applies under each drawing.

One to Remember

Have the entire class recite this poem using "rap" rhythm.

Once upon a time there was 1 sun,	$1 \times 1 = 1.$
Once upon a time there were 2 shoes,	$1 \times 2 = 2.$
One upon a time there were 3 trees,	$1 \times 3 = 3.$
Once upon a time there were 4 doors,	$1 \times 4 = 4.$
Once upon a time there were 5 knives,	$1 \times 5 = 5.$
Once upon a time there were 6 sticks,	$1 \times 6 = 6.$
Once upon a time there were 7 heavens,	$1 \times 7 = 7.$
Once upon a time there were 8 gates,	$1 \times 8 = 8.$
Once upon a time there were 9 vines,	$1 \times 9 = 9.$

Now divide the class into two groups. Instruct group one to "rap" the once-upon-a-time lines, alternating with group two chanting the "1 × 1 is 1" lines. Then see who has memorized the poem well enough to recite it by heart.

Multiplying by 2

You can introduce the concept of doubling by reading the following humorous folktale to your class.

Two of Everything

Mr. and Mrs. Yam had very little. They had a little home. They had a little garden. And in the garden, they had a little food. Mr. and Mrs. Yam had very little. But they were happy.

One day, Mr. Yam was digging in the garden. He struck something in the dirt. "What is this?" Mr. Yam asked.

Mr. Yam dug out a lot of dirt. What he saw surprised him. It was a huge pot.

"My, oh, my!" Mr. Yam cried. "What a big pot this is! I will take it to Mrs. Yam. She can cook food in it."

Mr. Yam carried the pot to his house. "What have you got there?" Mrs. Yam asked.

"This pot was in the yard," Mr. Yam said. "I think you can cook in it."

Mrs. Yam looked down into the big pot. A pin fell out of her hair. It fell into the pot. She put in her hand to take it out.

"Oh, my!" Mrs. Yam cried.

"What's wrong?" Mr. Yam asked.

"I put my hand in the pot to get my pin," Mrs. Yam explained. "But my hand came out with *two* pins! And both pins are exactly the same!"

"That cannot be so," said Mr. Yam. "One pin is not yours." But the two pins *did* look the same!

Mr. Yam looked down into the huge pot. His hat fell off. It fell into the big pot. Mr. Yam put in his hand to take it out. His hand came out with *two* hats! And both hats were the same!

"Oh, oh!" said Mr. Yam. "This pot is very funny. What goes in one, comes out two."

Mr. Yam took a dime. He dropped it into the pot. Then he put in his hand to take it out. He came out with *two* dimes!

Mr. and Mrs. Yam were very happy. They had found a lucky pot. It made two of everything.

Mr. and Mrs. Yam made up a song:

"A lucky pot for me and you! What goes in one, comes out two!"

Mr. Yam had an idea. "I will put some rice in the pot," he announced. "That way we will have more rice to eat."

Mrs. Yam looked at her husband. "Do we need all that rice?" she asked. "What if we cannot eat it all?"

"So what?" answered Mr. Yam. "It is good to have a lot." And so he put the rice in the pot. And the pot made two times as much rice!

"Oh, let us put in more things!" cried Mrs. Yam.

"Much more!" cried Mr. Yam.

And so they put in a mop. Out came two mops! They put in a fan. Out came two fans! They put in a rug. Out came two rugs!

Mr. and Mrs. Yam danced and sang: "A lucky pot for me and you! What goes in one, comes out two!"

The happy couple danced and sang for a long time.

"Oh, what fun this is!" Mr. Yam cried.

"Oh, how happy we are!" Mrs. Yam exclaimed.

"All thanks to our lucky pot," they both said.

Soon they were both tired. They had to sit down. Mr. and Mrs. Yam sat for a while.

Mrs. Yam said, "What can we put in the pot now?"

"Let me think," Mr. Yam said. "I think we have two of everything. What more do we need?"

Mr. and Mrs. Yam thought very hard. Then Mrs. Yam sat up.

"I have an idea!" she cried. "We have but one bed to sleep in. It is not very big. Let us put our bed into the pot. That way, we will have two beds!"

Mr. Yam said, "That is a good idea. But how can we put our bed into the pot? The pot is big, but it is not *that* big!"

"That is true," Mrs. Yam said. "But there is still a way we can do it. We will take the legs off the bed. We will put them in the pot. Then we will put in the mattress. Then we will put in the rest. If we push hard, it will all fit into the pot."

And so Mr. and Mrs. Yam went over to the bed. First they took off the legs and put them in the pot. Then they put in the mattress. Finally they tried fitting in the rest of the bed. But the bed was too big.

Mr. and Mrs. Yam pushed very, very hard. They tried to get the whole bed into the pot.

"Push! Push!" Mr. Yam cried.

"I am! I am!" Mrs. Yam cried back.

"Then push harder!" Mr. Yam said. "Keep pushing! Push! Push!"

Mr. and Mrs. Yam pushed as hard as they could. Suddenly they heard a loud CR-R-R-R-AAAACK!

The pot had cracked. It broke into two pieces.

"Oh, no! The pot is broken!" Mr. Yam cried.

"Oh, no! The pot is no more!" Mrs. Yam exclaimed.

"Can we fix it?" Mrs. Yam asked.

"I don't think so," Mr. Yam replied.

"No more lucky pot," they both sighed. "No more two of everything."

Mr. and Mrs. Yam looked at each other. They both looked very sad. Then Mr. Yam said, "Oh, well. We were lucky to have the pot at all. We did get two of a lot of things."

"That is true," Mrs. Yam agreed. "Maybe we don't need two of everything. Maybe we can be happy with what we have now."

"Yes," Mr. Yam nodded. "We were happy before having the pot. And we can be very, very happy now, too."

And so Mr. and Mrs. Yam put the pieces of their bed back together. And they were very happy with all that they had.

✓ FOR CLASS DISCUSSION: If you had a magic pot that made two of everything, what things would you like to put in it? Why?

Copycats

Another way to introduce the idea of doubling is through a visual game called Copycats. To play, invite one student to draw something on the board, such as 9 stars. Then have a second student, the "copycat," copy the design next to it.

Ask the class how many stars were on the board originally. How many are there now? Write the math sentence to express what has happened.

$$9 \times 2 = 18$$

Call on other volunteers to draw more designs (for example, 3 squares, 5 circles, 7 triangles, or 8 check marks). Then have your copycats do their work. Now help them write the appropriate math statement under each set of drawings.

Mirror, Mirror, on the Desk

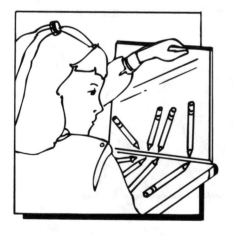

A student working alone can learn about doubling with the use of a small mirror. Have her place a number of like items on her desk, such as 4 pencils or 7 paper clips. Then ask her to hold a mirror in front of the items so she'll be able to see the reflected image. Have the student first guess how many items will be seen in all — meaning those on the desk *and* those in the mirror. Then have her count the items. Was her guess correct? Did 4 pencils become 8? Did 7 paper clips become 14? After each experiment, the student should write the math statement that expresses the problem.

$$4 \times 2 = 8 \qquad\qquad 7 \times 2 = 14$$

XXXXXXXXXXXXXXXXXXXXXXXXXXXXXX

Pair Pressure

See how many things your students can name that come in pairs. Write them on the board. The list might include:

- socks
- sneakers
- earrings
- earplugs
- roller skates
- contact lenses
- cuff links
- gloves
- leg warmers
- twins

Now tell your students silly word problems using the items on the list. For example:

- Eight cows bought contact lenses for themselves. How many lenses did they buy in all?

- Five elephants bought earrings for themselves. How many earrings did they buy in all?

- Three penguins bought cuff links for themselves. How many cuff links did they buy in all?

For each problem you give, have a volunteer come forward and draw a picture on the board illustrating the problem. Ask the student to write the multiplication sentence that expresses the problem underneath the picture.

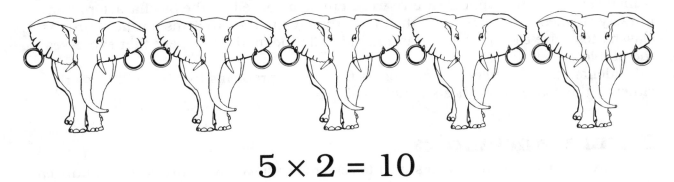

$$5 \times 2 = 10$$

A Song About 2s

Beginning with the 2s, this book provides songs for students to sing to learn multiples of numbers through 9. There is a different song for each number. The song about 2s can be found on page 38. You will also find suggestions for using the songs on page 40.

Multiplying by 3

For some reason, the number 3 has always been popular in nursery rhymes, folktales, jokes, and other story forms. Consider the three little pigs, the three bears, the three billy goats Gruff, and the three musketeers—not to mention, three blind mice and the three men in the tub. Try to come up with at least three more examples.

Silly Word Problems

You can capitalize on the popularity of 3 in children's stories by creating word problems based on them. For example:

The three bears had six pots of porridge apiece. How many pots did they have altogether?

$$6 \times 3 = 18$$

Each of the three little pigs bought five locks for his front door. How many locks did they buy in all?

$$5 \times 3 = 15$$

The three men in a tub each owned seven bars of soap. How many bars of soap did they own altogether?

$$7 \times 3 = 21$$

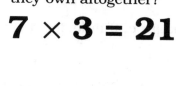

Each of the three blind mice had a cane. How many canes did they have in all?

$$1 \times 3 = 3$$

Invite students to invent their own word problems based on the 3s characters from nursery rhymes and stories, and then have them write the problems on the board. As classmates solve each problem, they should write the math statement that expresses the problem.

Students may draw pictures to express their story problems too. Have them work either at the board or on sheets of notebook paper.

Picture Mnemonics

Picture mnemonics often help students remember the answers to specific multiplication problems. Here are two picture mnemonics for multiplying by 3.

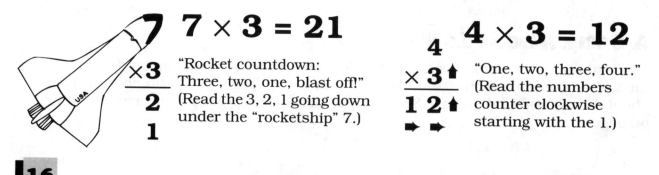

$$7 \times 3 = 21$$

"Rocket countdown: Three, two, one, blast off!" (Read the 3, 2, 1 going down under the "rocketship" 7.)

$$\begin{array}{r} 7 \\ \times 3 \\ \hline 2 \\ 1 \end{array}$$

$$4 \times 3 = 12$$

$$\begin{array}{r} 4 \\ \times 3 \\ \hline 1\,2 \end{array}$$

"One, two, three, four." (Read the numbers counter clockwise starting with the 1.)

The Breakfast Club

Since most of us eat three meals a day, counting meals is a practical way for students to learn multiples of three.

Use one week on a calendar as a visual aid when giving problems such as these:

• "Starting from Sunday morning, how many meals will you eat by the end of Wednesday evening?"

• "How many meals will you eat by the end of Saturday night?"

• "If you eat a slice of bread at every meal, how many slices will you eat after 5 days?"

• "If you drink a glass of milk at every meal, how many glasses will you drink in 6 days?

Super Challenge

• "How many meals have you eaten so far this month? This year?"

Tic-Tac-Toe with a Twist

The class can practice multiplying by 3 with this variation of tic-tac-toe. Begin by having students pair off. Distribute a copy of the game sheet below along with a copy of the Times Table on page 45 to each of the players. (Instruct students to keep the Times Table facedown and to refer to it only when checking answers.) In addition, have each duo make one set of nine index cards, numbered 1 to 9.

Players begin by shuffling the cards and turning them facedown on the desk.

Player A then turns over the top card. Player A must then multiply the number shown by a number on the board, and announce the product. (For example, "Three times eight is twenty-four.") If the player is correct, he covers the number 24 on the game sheet with a slip of paper bearing his initials. The card is set aside in a separate pile. If the answer is incorrect, the card is put at the bottom of the original pile.

Player B then draws a card and follows the same procedure. Players alternate turns. If either player covers three numbers on the game sheet going across, down, or diagonally, that person wins.

3	6	9
12	15	18
21	24	27

A Song About 3s

See page 38.

Multiplying by 4

When the three witches in *Macbeth* declared, "Double, double, toil and trouble," they had it all wrong. When it comes to multiplying by 4, "double, double" eliminates the trouble. How do you break this good news to students?

$$\begin{array}{r} 7 \\ \times 4 \\ \hline 28 \end{array}$$

Tell students that to multiply any number by 4, simply double the number and then add it to itself. Take 4×7, for example.

Double the 7 to get 14. Then add $14 + 14$ to get 28. It works like magic!

You can demonstrate this technique visually by writing the following on the chalkboard:

$$\begin{array}{r} 5 \\ \times 4 \\ \hline 20 \end{array} \qquad \begin{array}{r} 9 \\ \times 4 \\ \hline 36 \end{array} \qquad \begin{array}{r} 6 \\ \times 4 \\ \hline 24 \end{array} \qquad \begin{array}{r} 2 \\ \times 4 \\ \hline 8 \end{array}$$

$$\begin{array}{r} 3 \\ \times 4 \\ \hline 12 \end{array} \qquad \begin{array}{r} 8 \\ \times 4 \\ \hline 32 \end{array} \qquad \begin{array}{r} 4 \\ \times 4 \\ \hline 16 \end{array} \qquad \begin{array}{r} 1 \\ \times 4 \\ \hline 4 \end{array}$$

I've Got You Cornered

If your students went in search of the four corners of the earth, they'd have a hard time finding them. Even Christopher Columbus couldn't do it! But finding four corners on other things isn't as difficult.

Have students look around the room and identify objects with four corners. How about the door? The floor? The window? The poster? The chalkboard? The book?

Now challenge students to find *groups* of items having corners—for example, three books or seven posters. Ask, "How many corners do you see in the whole group?"

Three books will give them twelve corners.

Seven posters will give them twenty-eight corners.

For each group of items, have students touch and count the corners they see. Then have them write the appropriate multiplication statement.

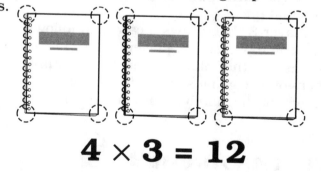

$$4 \times 3 = 12$$

A Corner Poem

How many students can memorize this poem for the 4s?
You may wish to duplicate this poem, so students can take it home to memorize it.

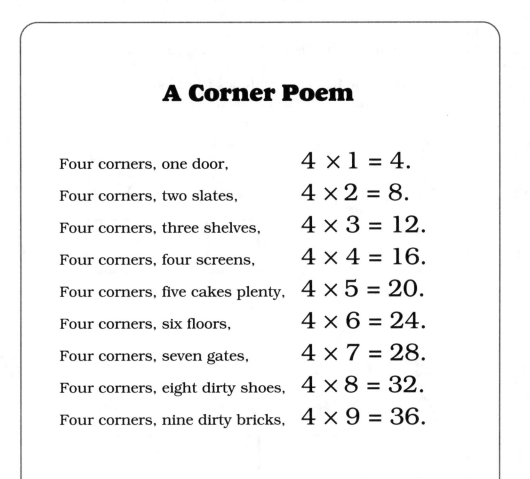

A Corner Poem

Four corners, one door,	$4 \times 1 = 4.$
Four corners, two slates,	$4 \times 2 = 8.$
Four corners, three shelves,	$4 \times 3 = 12.$
Four corners, four screens,	$4 \times 4 = 16.$
Four corners, five cakes plenty,	$4 \times 5 = 20.$
Four corners, six floors,	$4 \times 6 = 24.$
Four corners, seven gates,	$4 \times 7 = 28.$
Four corners, eight dirty shoes,	$4 \times 8 = 32.$
Four corners, nine dirty bricks,	$4 \times 9 = 36.$

A Song About 4s

See page 38.

Break the Code

Duplicate the puzzle on the next page for your students to work on at home.
(The answer is on page 62.)

Name:_____

Break the Code

You're a world-famous detective. You've cracked some of the toughest cases, and here's your latest assignment: Find out where animals who love the number 4 make their homes.

How do you do that?

First, do each of the 11 math problems below, writing your answers in the boxes beneath the problem.

Next, find the letter in the Code Key that matches the answer.

Now write the letter in the blank beneath the box.

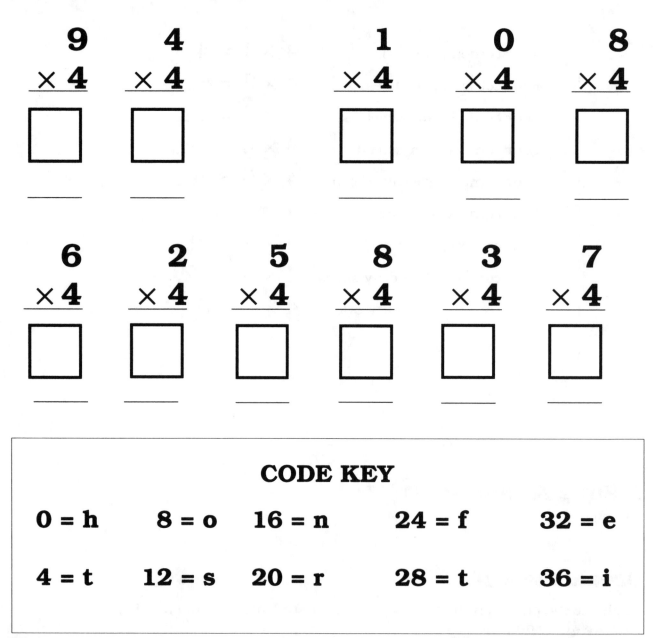

$$
\begin{array}{ccccc}
9 & 4 & 1 & 0 & 8 \\
\times 4 & \times 4 & \times 4 & \times 4 & \times 4
\end{array}
$$

$$
\begin{array}{cccccc}
6 & 2 & 5 & 8 & 3 & 7 \\
\times 4 & \times 4 & \times 4 & \times 4 & \times 4 & \times 4
\end{array}
$$

CODE KEY

0 = h	8 = o	16 = n	24 = f	32 = e
4 = t	12 = s	20 = r	28 = t	36 = i

Multiplying by 5

In general, students have little trouble remembering multiples of 5. This is largely because every product ends either in a 0 or a 5:

<u>5</u>   1<u>0</u>   1<u>5</u>   2<u>0</u>   2<u>5</u>   3<u>0</u>   3<u>5</u>   4<u>0</u>   4<u>5</u>

A good rule to make it even easier for students to remember their 5s is this:

| 5 | × | an even number | = | an answer ending in 0 |
| 5 | × | an odd number | = | an answer ending in 5 |

On the chalkboard, separate the odds from the evens to show how this works.

EVENS:	0	2	4	6	8
	×5	×5	×5	×5	×5
	0	10	20	30	40
ODDS:	1	3	5	7	9
	×5	×5	×5	×5	×5
	5	15	25	35	45

To Halve and Halve Not

Here's a simple trick for multiplying by 5 that many kids will find helpful.

1. Write 0 after the number being multiplied by 5.
2. Divide that number in half.

For example, to solve 5×8:

1. Write 0 after the 8. That makes 80.
2. Divide 80 in half. That's 40.

Students who are able to halve numbers quickly will find this trick invaluable. It can also be used to multiply larger numbers by 5 as well. For example, 5×365.

1. Write 0 after the 365. That makes 3,650.
2. Divide 3,650 in half. That's 1,825.

Try several examples with your students. Most of your students will get the knack in no time.

A Song About 5s

See page 38.

Five Fill-In

Duplicate the exercise on the next page and distribute one to each student. (The answer is on page 62.)

Name:_____

5 Fill-in

1. Solve each problem at the left.

2. On the same line, color in the box with the correct answer.

3. When you're done, tilt your paper on its side to the left.

4. You will see how to write 5 in Roman numerals.

$3 \times 5 =$ ___

10	25	40	0	15

$7 \times 5 =$ ___

5	15	25	35	20

$4 \times 5 =$ ___

30	5	20	10	40

$2 \times 5 =$ ___

45	10	25	40	15

$8 \times 5 =$ ___

40	30	25	5	0

$1 \times 5 =$ ___

15	5	0	20	35

$5 \times 5 =$ ___

40	20	25	15	5

$9 \times 5 =$ ___

0	5	30	45	15

$6 \times 5 =$ ___

10	5	35	15	30

Multiplying by 6

When you teach multiplication by 6, introduce students to the family known as the Sick Sixes. Use paper dolls as visual aids.

There are six members in the household: Sid, Sybil, Cindy, Cyril, Sylvia, and Sigmund. Sad to say, the Sick Sixes are always getting sick. They come down with everything from colds to stomachaches. And they all get sick at the same time.

Luckily, the Sick Sixes have a family doctor who gives them special medicine. Since they all have the same illness, they all need the same medicine.

For example, when the family has runny noses, the doctor tells each family member to take 2 spoonfuls of Slurp Syrup.

So how many spoonfuls do they take in all?

Use plastic spoons to demonstrate. Place two spoons in front of each doll. Have the class count the total number of spoons.

| Sid | Sybil | Cindy | Cyril | Sylvia | Sigmund |

Write this statement on the board:

$$2 \times 6 = 12$$

Have students arrange more plastic spoons to solve these problems:

• When the family has stomachaches, the doctor orders each person to take five spoonfuls of Stomach Tonic. How many spoonfuls is that in all?

• When the family has itchy elbows, the doctor orders each person to take nine spoonfuls of Itch Mix. How many spoonfuls is that in all?

• When the family has ticklish tongues, the doctor orders each person to take one spoonful of No-Tickle Pickle Juice. How many spoonfuls is that in all?

With each case you give, have the appropriate multiplication statement written on the board.

Six and Shout

Some multiples of 6 end with the same digit as the number being multiplied by 6. For example, 6 times <u>4</u> is 2<u>4</u>. Children may remember these multiples by stressing the matching numbers.

"Six times FOUR is twenty-FOUR!"
"Six times SIX is thirty-SIX!"
"Six times EIGHT is forty-EIGHT!"

The Role of the Dice

Now that your class has completed multiplication through 6, you can turn an ordinary pair of dice into an educational tool.

Give a pair of dice to every two students, along with a copy of the reproducible Times Table on page 45. Instruct students to keep the Times Table facedown and refer to it only when checking answers. One student rolls the dice. When the two numbers come up (3 and 6, for example), the student multiplies them and announces the product. Then his partner rolls. Students may compete to see who is first to call out the correct product each time.

For a somewhat more involved game, distribute a copy of the Role-of-the-Dice Grid on the following page to each student.

Player A of each team rolls the dice and multiplies the numbers. If her answer is correct, she writes the product in the corresponding box on the grid. For example, if 6 and 6 were rolled, she would write 36 in the lower right corner of her grid. If her answer is wrong, she forfeits the chance to fill in her grid on that turn.

Player B then rolls and follows the same procedure. Both players continue to roll, alternating turns.

If a player rolls a combination she has rolled previously, she fills in nothing and the next player takes her turn.

The first player to fill in her entire grid wins the game.

$4 \times 3 = 12$

$1 \times 6 = 6$

Name:_____

The Role of the Dice

×	1	2	3	4	5	6
1						
2						
3						
4						
5						
6						

The Domino Effect

What can be done with dice can also be done, in some variation, with dominoes. A domino has two halves, and each half has dots totaling 0 to 6; so students then can use a domino much like they use a pair of dice.

After students pair off, have them spread a set of dominoes facedown on a desk. Player A turns over any domino, multiplies the two numbers, and announces the product. (A blank represents 0.) The domino is kept facedown afterward. Then player B turns over another domino and does the same thing. They play until all dominoes are faceup.

Students may fill in a grid during the game, as they did with the dice; however, they must add a column for the number 0.

When the grid is used to play, all dominoes are placed facedown. Player A turns one up, multiplies the two numbers, and enters the correct product in his grid. He then turns the domino facedown and places it somewhere on the table, while player B keeps his eyes closed.

Player B then takes his turn, following the same procedure. The first player to fill his entire grid wins the game.

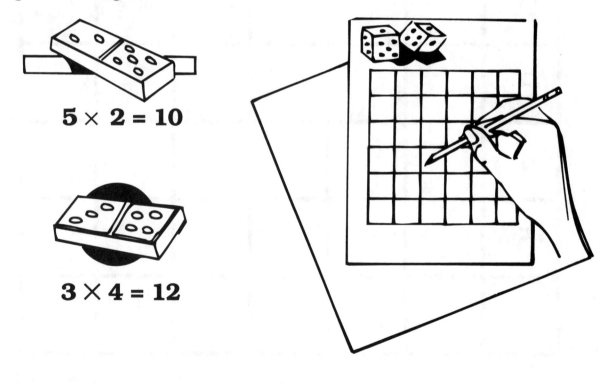

$5 \times 2 = 10$

$3 \times 4 = 12$

A Song About 6s

See page 39.

XXXXXXXXXXXXXXXXXXXXXXXXXX

Multiplying by 7

When your class is ready to learn to multiply by 7, it's time to kick in with some fun visualization techniques. Since football teams score 7 points at a time, students may find it easy to think of the number 7 as a football player wearing shoulder pads.

These two 7s play for the Forty-niners.

$$7 \times 7 = 49$$

Picture 6 as the player's girlfriend. On a date, 7 and 6 see a movie on 42nd Street.

$$7 \times 6 = 42$$

Have the students work as a class to come up with other clever mnemonics from the world of football for multiples of 7.

A mnemonic for 7×8, unrelated to football, focuses on the number sequence 5-6-7-8.

$$56 = 7 \times 8$$

What's the Score?

Since the final scores of football games are often multiples of 7, kids can enjoy playing What's the Score? to review multiplication by 7.

Have pairs of students number a set of 9 cards from 1 to 9 and then shuffle them. Each player draws a card and multiplies his number by 7 to get his team's final score.

The cards are shuffled again, and players draw again. Have them calculate as many "final scores" as they wish.

A Song About the 7s

See page 39.

'Mazing Seven

Duplicate the game board on the following page. Distribute one to each student. (The answer is on page 62.)

'Mazing Seven

Make a path through the multiples of 7 in order, from start to finish. Try to reach the finish without entering any incorrect boxes.

START

7	6	21	16	9	15
20	14	16	28	25	12
29	26	30	35	36	31
38	22	40	39	42	44
46	32	37	49	43	47
50	54	45	53	56	59
62	68	52	60	65	63

FINISH

Multiplying by 8

Who multiplies by 8 more than Oliver Octopus? Introduce your students to Oliver by drawing his picture on the board.

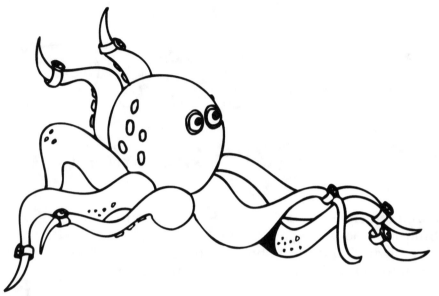

Now give the following word problem to the class:

Oliver Octopus wears one watch on each of his arms. How many watches does he wear in all?

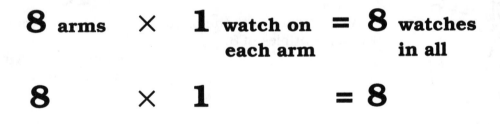

8 arms × **1** watch on each arm = **8** watches in all

8 × **1** = **8**

Have a student draw the eight watches on the board. Then have the student write a multiplication statement to express the problem.

Try these other word problems with the class:

1. Oliver has five fake fingernails on the tip of each arm. How many fake finger nails does he have in all?
2. Oliver has nine dimples on each arm. How many dimples in all?
3. Oliver has four bracelets on each arm. How many bracelets in all?
4. Oliver has six freckles on each arm. How many freckles in all?
5. Oliver has eight hairs on each arm. How many hairs in all?
6. Oliver has three snails crawling on each arm. How many snails in all?
7. Oliver has two bandaids on each arm. How many bandaids in all?
8. Oliver has seven spots on each arm. How many spots in all?

You Must Remember This

Here's a picture that will cause a chuckle while it helps students to remember that $3 \times 8 = 24$:

The **3** little pigs ate **(8)** = **24** tons of apples.

To help children remember that $6 \times 8 = 48$, tell them to picture Mrs. Smith's famous tea party:

Six people were invited, but eight showed up. Mrs. Smith didn't seem to mind, though. She just set the table for eight!

$$\begin{array}{r} 6 \\ \times\,\underline{8} \\ 48 \end{array}$$

Adding rhymes to the picture trick is a great way to teach other mutiples of 8:

Skate, skate, figure eights
all the way to the shore—
8 times 8 is 64.

$$\begin{array}{r} 8 \\ \times\,\underline{8} \\ 64 \end{array}$$

Another rhyme children enjoy:

8 times 8 is 64,
Shut your mouth
and say no more.

A Song About 8s

See page 39.

Multiplying by 9

Finger multiplication for the 9s is far less involved than it is for the 6s, 7s, and 8s. Here's how to do it:

Have children hold out their hands, palms down. Each finger is given a number from 1 to 10, starting from the left.

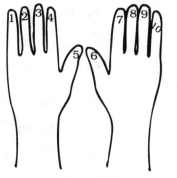

Suppose students wish to multiply 9 by 4. They simply tuck under finger number 4. That leaves three fingers to the left of it and six fingers to the right of it, which stands for 36. 9 × 4 = 36.

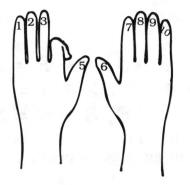

Here's another example. For 9 times 8, children tuck under finger number 8. This leaves seven fingers to the left of it and two fingers to the right of it, or 72. 9 × 8 = 72.

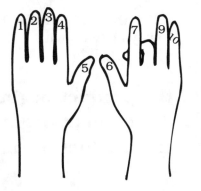

Have students use this method to multiply other numbers between 1 and 9 by 9. It works every time. And no batteries are required.

It All Adds Up...to Nine

There are other "tricks" about the 9s that students will appreciate. Write the following on the board:

$$9 \times 1 = 9$$
$$9 \times 2 = 18$$
$$9 \times 3 = 27$$
$$9 \times 4 = 36$$
$$9 \times 5 = 45$$
$$9 \times 6 = 54$$
$$9 \times 7 = 63$$
$$9 \times 8 = 72$$
$$9 \times 9 = 81$$

Have students study the column of products at the far right. Point out that the digits in each answer always add up to 9.

For example:

with 18, 1 + 8 = 9
with 27, 2 + 7 = 9
with 36, 3 + 6 = 9

Have students add the digits in the remaining products to make sure the rule applies. Students can use this procedure to verify that a product they have calculated is correct.

It's Always One Less

Students may notice another peculiar thing about the 9s products.

Starting with 9×2, the product always begins with a digit that is *one less* than the number being multiplied by 9.

For example:

with 9×2, the product begins with a $\underline{1}$.
with 9×3, the product begins with a $\underline{2}$.
with 9×8, the product begins with a $\underline{7}$.

Knowing this, students merely figure out what digit must be added to the first to achieve a total of 9. They now have both digits of the product.

XXXXXXXXXXXXXXXXXXXXXXXXXX

Putting It Together

Here's a puzzle your class will enjoy piecing together, using their 9s table to help them.

Begin by taking a full-page picture from a magazine. The picture should be of a face, a house, or something that will look funny if it's not in the right order. Paste a sheet of white paper on the back of the picture. Draw lines to divide the white paper into twelve squares, as shown below. Then write the problems as shown.

Now cut along the lines so you end up with twelve squares. Shuffle them and lay them out, picture-side down, in a straight line. Challenge your students to arrange the squares so the multiplication problems and their answers appear in the right order. Once the squares are in place, have students turn them over. If they've arranged the squares correctly, they'll see your original magazine photo.

9 ×3 **27**	9 ×6 **54**	9 ×1 **9**
9 ×9 **81**	9 ×7 **63**	9 ×8 **72**
9 ×5 **45**	9 ×2 **18**	9 ×4 **36**

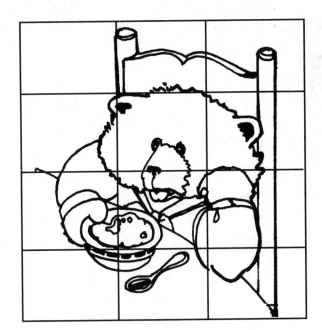

Super Challenge

Here's a 9s brainteaser that's trickier than it seems:

How many times does the digit 9 appear in whole numbers between 1 and 100? Most students answer "Ten," because they count:

"9, 19, 29, 39, 49, 59, 69, 79, 89, 99."

Other students answer "Eleven," because they remember that 99 has two nines in it.

However, both answers are wrong. The correct answer is 20. Many people simply forget to count 90, 91, 92, 93, and so on.

A Song About 9s

See page 39.

Multiplying by 10

Multiplying any number by 10 may be the easiest operation students learn. The rule is simple: Just add a zero at the end of the number being multiplied by 10.

$$10 \times \underline{6} = \underline{6}0 \qquad\qquad 10 \times \underline{2} = \underline{2}0$$

You can use manipulatives to show why this works. For example, take three paper clips and place them on a table in a group. Then ask for a volunteer to make nine more groups of three clips. Count the total number of clips. Write the multiplication sentence that expresses what has happened.

$$10 \times \underline{3} = \underline{3}0$$

Have other volunteers follow the same procedure, making ten groups of five clips then ten groups of eight clips, and so on. Each time, have a student write the multiplication sentence on the board.

$$10 \times \underline{5} = \underline{5}0 \qquad\qquad 10 \times \underline{8} = \underline{8}0$$

Your students will enjoy discovering that they now have the ability to multiply any number, no matter how large, by 10. No matter what the number, they merely add 0 to the end.

$$10 \times \underline{28} = \underline{28}0 \qquad 10 \times \underline{396} = \underline{3,96}0$$

$$10 \times \underline{6,748,329} = \underline{67,483,29}0$$

Rave Review

Congratulations! Your students have completed their "times tables" through the 10s. Now is a good time to review some of those tables with them.

The beauty of this activity is that it's not a rote drill. It's a creative way of multiplying the 6s through the 9s—even if students remember only the 1s through 4s!

Any number between 6 and 9 can be multiplied by any other number between 6 and 9, using only the multiplication tables up to 4.

Here's how:

Say you want to multiply 9 × 6. Write the two numbers like this:

9

6

Next, subtract each number from 10, and write the difference of each at the right.

(10 - 9 = 1)

(10 - 6 = 4)

Now, to find the tens digit for the product of 9 × 6, subtract diagonally. You may subtract either 4 from 9 or 1 from 6. Either way, the difference will be 5. Hence, the tens digit will be 5.

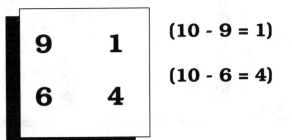

(9 - 4 = 5)

or

(6 - 1 = 5)

To find the ones digit for the product, multiply the two numbers at the right—in this case, 4 and 1. Since 4 × 1 = 4, the ones digit is 4. Hence, 9 × 6 = 54.

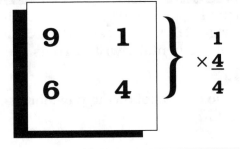

Why does this system work? Since you're multiplying only the 6s, 7s, and 9s, the highest possible digit to appear in the right column will be 4 (that is, 10 - 6). Thus the final step of this procedure requires knowledge of multiplication only up to 4.

Here's another example: What's the product of 8 × 7?

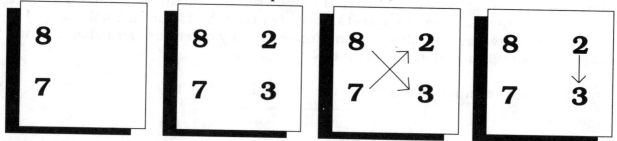

First, write the two numbers in the left-hand corners of the box. Then subtract each number from 10, and write the difference at the right. Next, subtract diagonally to get the tens digit (in this case 5). Finally, multiply the two numbers in the right column (in this case 2 × 3) to get the ones digit. Hence, 8 × 7 = 56.

Give students more problems for practicing this procedure:

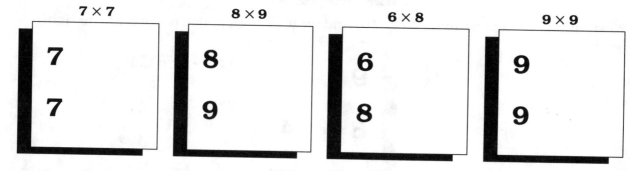

A Few Exceptions

In the cases of 6 × 6 and 6 × 7, students will find a slightly different calculation is required. Take 6 × 6, for example.

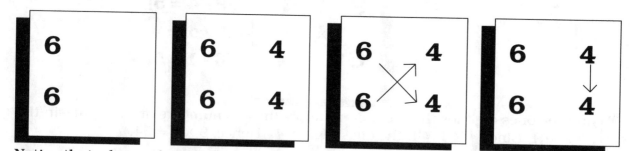

Notice that when subtracting diagonally, the tens digit comes out to 2. When students multiply 4 × 4, they get 16. In this case, the 16 must be added to 20 to get 36. Make sure students do not accidentally write 216 as the product.

Pattern Search

Make a copy of the puzzle on the following page for each student.
(The answer is on page 62.)

Pattern Search

Hidden in the puzzle are the number patterns for multiples of numbers 1 to 9.
For example, somewhere in the puzzle is the series 4, 8, 12, 16, 20, 24, 28, 32, 36. Each
pattern may run across or down.

Can you find all 9 patterns? Circle each pattern as you discover it.
Try using different colored pencils for a rainbow effect.

4	8	2	4	6	8	10	12	14	16	18	5	12
1	9	12	3	32	72	6	7	8	18	21	8	63
2	10	9	6	4	8	12	16	20	24	28	32	36
3	7	16	9	40	49	18	28	21	30	35	9	81
4	32	12	12	8	16	24	32	40	48	56	64	72
5	5	10	15	20	25	30	35	40	45	48	18	40
6	24	20	18	49	81	36	40	81	35	20	28	21
7	7	14	21	28	35	42	49	56	63	9	42	4
8	18	16	24	63	21	48	64	72	64	6	35	2
9	9	18	27	36	45	54	63	72	81	2	16	18

Musical Multiples (Songs) 🏠

Most children learn their ABCs to the tune of "Twinkle, Twinkle, Little Star." So why not learn the multiplication tables with music as well?

Each of the popular songs introduced on these pages can help students remember the multiples of the numbers 2 through 9.

For the 2s (sung to "If You're Happy and You Know It")

Two, four, six, eight, ten, twelve, four - teen, six - teen, eighteen.
If you're hap - py and you know it, clap your hands.

For the 3s (sung to "This Land Is Your Land")

Three, six, nine, twel - ve, fif - teen, eight - teen,
This land is your land, this land is my land,

Twenty - one, twenty-four, twen-ty - se - ven, thir - ty.
From Cal - i - for nia to the New York Is - land.

For the 4s (sung to "Old MacDonald Had a Farm")

Four, eight, twelve, six - teen, twen - ty, twen - ty-four,
Old Mac Don - ald had a farm, E - I - E - I - O.

Twen - ty - eight, thir - ty - two, thir - ty - six, forty.
And on this farm he had a cow, E - I - E - I - O.

For the 5s (sung to "I've Got Sixpence")

Five, ten, fif - teen, twen - ty, twen - ty - five,
I've got six - pence, jol - ly jol - ly six - pence,

Thirty, thirty - five, for - ty, for - ty - five.
I've got six - pence to last me all my life.

For the 6s (sung to "You Are My Sunshine")

Six, twelve, eight - teen, twenty- four, thir - ty,
You are my sunshine, my only sun - shine,

Thirty - six, forty-two, forty-eight, fifty-four.
You make me happy when skies are gray.

For the 7s (sung to "Happy Birthday to You")

Sev - en, four - teen, twenty - one, twen- ty - eight, thirty-five,
Hap - py birth - day to you, hap - py birth - day to you,

For - ty - two, forty - nine, fif - ty - six, sixty-three.
Hap - py birth - day to you, hap - py birth - day to you.

For the 8s (sung to "She'll Be Comin' Round the Mountain")

Eight, six - teen, twen - ty - four, thir - ty - two, for - ty,
She'll be com - in' round the mountain when she comes, (when she comes).

For - ty - eight, fif - ty - six, six - ty - four, seventy - two.
She'll be com - in' round the mountain when she comes, (when she comes).

For the 9s (sung to "The Star-Spangled Banner")

Nine, eight - teen, twenty - seven, thir - ty - six, for - ty - five,
O, say can you see by the dawn's ear - ly light,

Fif - ty - four, six - ty - three, seven - ty - two, eight - y - one.
What so proud - ly we hailed at the twi - light's last gleaming.

How to Use the Songs

Knowing all the multiples of a particular number, such as 7, can help children remember a specific problem, such as 7 × 5.

The child sings the 7 song, counting the numbers on his fingers along the way: "Seven, fourteen, twenty-one, twenty-eight, thirty-five." The child stops on the fifth number counted—35. Hence, 7 × 5 is 35.

There are other activities students may do once they've learned a song. Take nine slips of paper and write the multiples of a number. For example:

7	14	21	28	35	42	49	54	63

A student turns over all the slips so the numbers are facedown. To check the answer for the problem 7 × 3, she sings the song to the third number, announces the product, and then verifies her answer by turning over the slip of paper.

The student repeats this procedure with every number until all the slips of paper have been turned over.

In a variation of this activity, start with all the slips of paper faceup. Cover up a particular number. See if the student can name the number by using the song as an aid.

Pairs of students can also play Name That Product. One student begins singing one of the songs and stops wherever he wishes. The other student must then say (or sing) the number that comes next in the song.

Easy-Does-It Chart

Learning all the multiplication tables through 9 may seem like an impossible task to some children. But if problems are organized in the manner below, the job may seem less daunting.

Children usually learn their 0's, 1s, and 2s quickly. They know the 5s end in either a 5 or a 0. The 9s can be solved with various tricks they have learned, such as finger-counting. The "doubles" (4 × 4 or 3 × 3, for example) somehow become easier to remember when learned together.

That leaves only the "last ten" — the ten problems that are the toughest to learn. If children can master these, then they're home free.

Make a copy of the sheet on the following page for each student to complete.

Name: _____

Easy-Does-It Chart

×0, ×1	×5	×9	Doubles
0 × 2 = _____	5 × 5 = _____	9 × 9 = _____	4 × 4 = _____
1 × 3 = _____	5 × 7 = _____	9 × 2 = _____	6 × 6 = _____
0 × 1 = _____	5 × 1 = _____	9 × 8 = _____	5 × 5 = _____
1 × 4 = _____	5 × 6 = _____	9 × 1 = _____	7 × 7 = _____
0 × 3 = _____	5 × 4 = _____	9 × 6 = _____	9 × 9 = _____
1 × 5 = _____	5 × 8 = _____	9 × 3 = _____	8 × 8 = _____
0 × 5 = _____	5 × 3 = _____	9 × 7 = _____	3 × 3 = _____
1 × 7 = _____	5 × 9 = _____	9 × 5 = _____	1 × 1 = _____
1 × 9 = _____	5 × 2 = _____	9 × 4 = _____	2 × 2 = _____

×0, ×1	Last Ten		×2
0 × 6 = _____			
0 × 8 = _____			2 × 7 = _____
1 × 8 = _____	4 × 6 = _____	3 × 6 = _____	2 × 5 = _____
1 × 6 = _____	7 × 4 = _____	8 × 6 = _____	2 × 2 = _____
0 × 9 = _____	3 × 7 = _____	6 × 7 = _____	2 × 4 = _____
1 × 2 = _____	8 × 4 = _____	7 × 8 = _____	2 × 6 = _____
0 × 0 = _____	4 × 3 = _____	3 × 8 = _____	2 × 3 = _____
0 × 4 = _____			2 × 9 = _____
1 × 1 = _____			2 × 1 = _____
			2 × 8 = _____

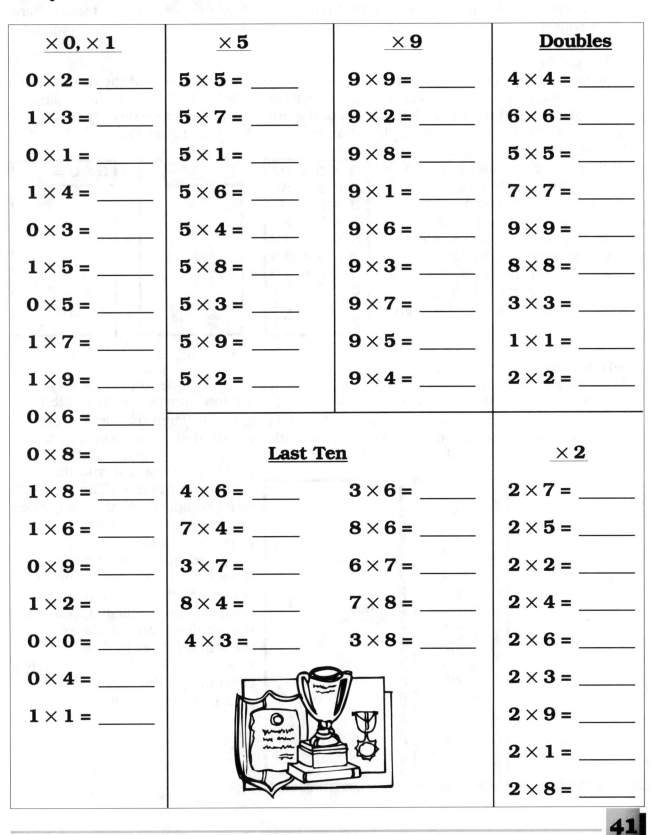

Homemade Practice Cards

Multiplication drill cards are a tried-and-true method for memorizing the tables. Here are two ways for your students to make them using scissors, index cards, and paper.

1. Slide Cards

Students will need two index cards to begin. On card A, they write all the multiplication problems for any number between 1 and 9 (See figure A below). Students then take scissors and cut out the upper left portion of the other card, so it reveals only the first problem but not the answer when placed on top of card A. (See figure C).

To use, students lay card B over card A and give the answer to the problem that is visible. They then slide card B down one line so the answer appears and the next problem becomes visible. Students repeat the procedure for all problems appearing on card A.

A separate index card should be prepared for each number between 1 and 9.

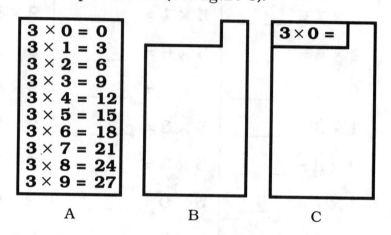

$$3 \times 0 = 0$$
$$3 \times 1 = 3$$
$$3 \times 2 = 6$$
$$3 \times 3 = 9$$
$$3 \times 4 = 12$$
$$3 \times 5 = 15$$
$$3 \times 6 = 18$$
$$3 \times 7 = 21$$
$$3 \times 8 = 24$$
$$3 \times 9 = 27$$

$$3 \times 0 =$$

A   B   C

2. Window Sheets

For this activity, students will need a sheet of construction paper, a piece of plain white paper, and scissors. Instruct them to cut out a window approximately $2\frac{1}{2}$ inches by $\frac{1}{2}$ inch in the middle of the construction paper (see figure D). Then tell them to cut a strip of the white paper approximately 2 inches wide and 10 inches long. On the strip, have them write all the multiplication problems for any number between 1 and 9—the problem on one line and the answer on the next. The lines must be spaced so that only one line appears in the window at a time. (See figure E.)

To use, students simply slip the strip into the construction paper (see figure F) and adjust until the top problem appears in the window. After students give the answer, they pull the strip upward to see if it's correct. They continue pulling upward for the next problem and answer.

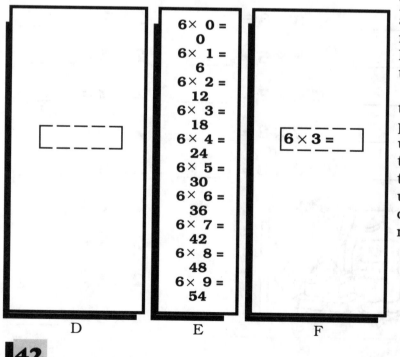

$$6 \times 0 =$$
$$0$$
$$6 \times 1 =$$
$$6$$
$$6 \times 2 =$$
$$12$$
$$6 \times 3 =$$
$$18$$
$$6 \times 4 =$$
$$24$$
$$6 \times 5 =$$
$$30$$
$$6 \times 6 =$$
$$36$$
$$6 \times 7 =$$
$$42$$
$$6 \times 8 =$$
$$48$$
$$6 \times 9 =$$
$$54$$

$$6 \times 3 =$$

D   E   F

XXXXXXXXXXXXXXXXXXXXXXXXXXX

Real-Life Multiplication

For some children, knowing when to use multiplication to solve a word problem can be a challenge in itself. The following checklist can help them decide. Make a copy for each student.

WHEN DO I MULTIPLY?

1. Does the problem ask me to find the total amount?

2. Do I see words like *in all*, *altogether*, or *total*?

Now give your class these real-life word problems to solve. Have them identify the key words that indicate that multiplication is required.

1. At the start of the school year, you want to buy pencils. You use five pencils every month. There are nine months of school. How many pencils will you need in all?

2. Three classmates are having birthday parties in school. You are in charge of bringing candles for their cakes. If each cake needs nine candles, how many candles do you need altogether?

3. It's your turn to bring snacks to class. You can't remember how many children are in your class. But you know there are six rows of desks, and there are six desks per row. How many snacks should you bring altogether?

4. At the arcade, computer games cost fifty cents each. You have four dollars in your pocket, which you have saved for several weeks. A dollar, as you know, is worth four quarters, and there are two quarters in fifty cents. How many games can you play in all?

(The answers to these problems are on page 62.)

Special Challenge

Hot dogs are sold 8 to a package. Hot dog buns, on the other hand, are sold 10 to a package. How many packages of hot dogs and how many packages of buns must you buy to come out with the same total number of each?

The Table Is Set

On the next page, you'll find a times table showing all the products of the 0's through the 9s, which will be an invaluable reference for children. Make one copy for each student or copy the table on a large piece of chart paper and display it on the classroom wall. On pages 46 and 47, there are two more tables that will put your students to the ultimate test. Make a copy of each for your students to work on in class or at home. (The answer to What's Wrong with This Table is on page 62.)

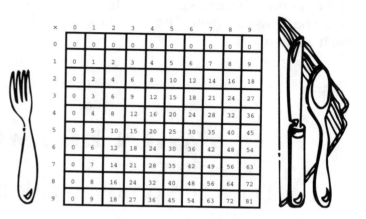

x	0	1	2	3	4	5	6	7	8	9
0	0	0	0	0	0	0	0	0	0	0
1	0	1	2	3	4	5	6	7	8	9
2	0	2	4	6	8	10	12	14	16	18
3	0	3	6	9	12	15	18	21	24	27
4	0	4	8	12	16	20	24	28	32	36
5	0	5	10	15	20	25	30	35	40	45
6	0	6	12	18	24	30	36	42	48	54
7	0	7	14	21	28	35	42	49	56	63
8	0	8	16	24	32	40	48	56	64	72
9	0	9	18	27	36	45	54	63	72	81

Marvelous Multiplication Reproducibles

Looking for an entertaining way to reinforce your students' multiplication skills? On the following pages, you'll find seven reproducible activities especially designed to do just that.

Choose from:

(You'll find the answers to all of these puzzles on pages 63 and 64.)

Name:_____

The Times Table

To use the table, simply find the two numbers you are multiplying, taking one from the top row, and the other from the row running down the left side.

Now run your fingers down and across from these numbers. The product will appear where your fingers meet.

✕	0	1	2	3	4	5	6	7	8	9
0	0	0	0	0	0	0	0	0	0	0
1	0	1	2	3	4	5	6	7	8	9
2	0	2	4	6	8	10	12	14	16	18
3	0	3	6	9	12	15	18	21	24	27
4	0	4	8	12	16	20	24	28	32	36
5	0	5	10	15	20	25	30	35	40	45
6	0	6	12	18	24	30	36	42	48	54
7	0	7	14	21	28	35	42	49	56	63
8	0	8	16	24	32	40	48	56	64	72
9	0	9	18	27	36	45	54	63	72	81

Name:_____

Set the Table Yourself!

The multiplication table below is incomplete. Fill in the missing products.

×	0	1	2	3	4	5	6	7	8	9
0										
1										
2							12			
3										
4										
5										
6										
7										
8				24						
9										

Name:_____

What's Wrong with This Table?

Below is a multiplication table in which some products are incorrect. Can you find them? As you go along, color in the boxes that show incorrect products.

Bonus: There's a surprise message in store for those who find them all.

×	0	1	2	3	4	5	6	7	8	9
0	0	0	0	0	0	0	0	0	0	0
1	0	1	2	3	4	5	6	7	8	9
2	2	3	6	7	8	11	12	14	15	18
3	2	3	6	10	12	16	18	20	24	27
4	4	4	8	13	16	21	25	28	32	36
5	5	5	10	16	20	26	30	36	40	45
6	3	0	13	16	24	8	36	42	46	54
7	0	7	14	21	28	35	42	49	56	63
8	0	8	16	24	32	40	48	56	64	72
9	0	9	18	27	36	45	54	63	72	81

Name:_____

Problem Hunt

There are twenty-four multiplication problems hidden in the puzzle below. See how many you can find. The problems may read across or down. Circle the problems—and their answers—as you spot them. Fill in the × sign and the = sign for each.

Two problems have already been circled to get you started.

4	6	24	9	16	3	8	24	5	0
5	7	36	3	3	6	18	72	8	6
8	2	2	27	22	9	7	9	40	0
2	14	2	12	5	8	4	6	20	7
16	28	4	0	2	72	1	54	7	6
1	7	7	9	10	32	4	50	× 5	49
8 × 6 = 48			4	38	2	9	18	35	63
5	7	5	36	7	7	49	0	7	3
0	19	6	9	33	3	4	12	8	5
0	14	30	1	2	88	5	66	56	15

Name:_____

The Same But Different

Find the two problems in each row whose product is the same as the product shown at the left. Now write the letters in that same order in the blanks at the bottom of the page. The word you spell will tell you who you are.

18 =	$\begin{array}{r}3\\ \times6\\ \hline M\end{array}$	$\begin{array}{r}4\\ \times5\\ \hline E\end{array}$	$\begin{array}{r}2\\ \times9\\ \hline U\end{array}$	$\begin{array}{r}7\\ \times3\\ \hline S\end{array}$
12 =	$\begin{array}{r}3\\ \times3\\ \hline A\end{array}$	$\begin{array}{r}2\\ \times6\\ \hline L\end{array}$	$\begin{array}{r}3\\ \times4\\ \hline T\end{array}$	$\begin{array}{r}9\\ \times3\\ \hline H\end{array}$
24 =	$\begin{array}{r}3\\ \times8\\ \hline I\end{array}$	$\begin{array}{r}6\\ \times3\\ \hline C\end{array}$	$\begin{array}{r}3\\ \times5\\ \hline A\end{array}$	$\begin{array}{r}6\\ \times4\\ \hline P\end{array}$
36 =	$\begin{array}{r}9\\ \times3\\ \hline B\end{array}$	$\begin{array}{r}6\\ \times6\\ \hline L\end{array}$	$\begin{array}{r}4\\ \times4\\ \hline Y\end{array}$	$\begin{array}{r}9\\ \times4\\ \hline I\end{array}$
16 =	$\begin{array}{r}4\\ \times4\\ \hline E\end{array}$	$\begin{array}{r}2\\ \times8\\ \hline R\end{array}$	$\begin{array}{r}7\\ \times4\\ \hline S\end{array}$	$\begin{array}{r}9\\ \times7\\ \hline H\end{array}$

You are ____ ____ ____ ____ ____ ____ ____ ____ ____

Name:_____

The Secret Message

Inside each brick, write the answer to the problem.
If the answer is 29 or less, color the brick red.
If the answer is 30 or more, color the brick green.
If all your answers are right, a hidden message will appear!
It will tell you the name of a multiplier's favorite newspaper.

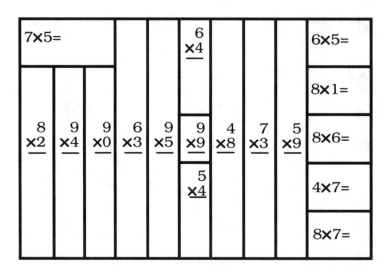

What's Dot?

Write the answer to each multiplication problem. Then draw lines connecting the dots in the same order as your answers.

What do you see?

1. **2 × 8 =**

2. **6 × 4 =**

3. **5 × 5 =**

4. **8 × 9 =**

5. **5 × 8 =**

6. **8 × 8 =**

7. **5 × 3 =**

8. **9 × 4 =**

9. **8 × 3 =**

10. **4 × 4 =**

11. **7 × 4 =**

12. **6 × 2 =**

13. **4 × 8 =**

14. **6 × 7 =**

15. **9 × 6 =**

16. **6 × 6 =**

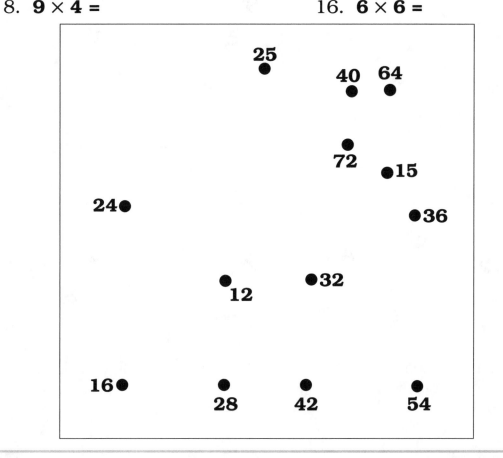

Number Jumbles

Some boxes filled with multiplication problems fell off the back of a truck. Uh-oh! Now all the numbers are jumbled.

Put things back in order. Rearrange the numbers in each box to make a multiplication problem. The first box has been done.

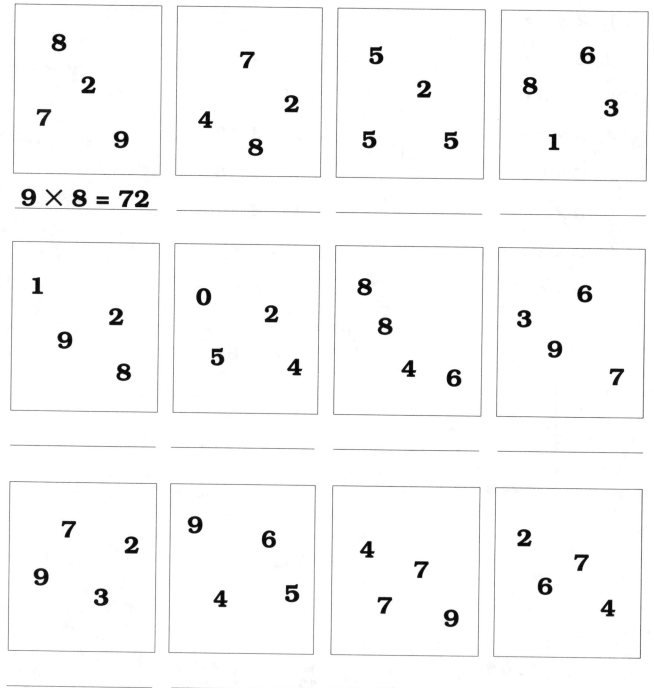

$9 \times 8 = 72$

Name:_____

Magic Squares

What's magic about a magic square? In multiplication, it's the way different numbers in a large square work together. Somehow the different rows of numbers "magically" produce the same product in the corner.

To the right is an example:

Now here are some problems for you to work on. Complete each magic square with the right numbers, so that the problems work going across and down. Good Luck!

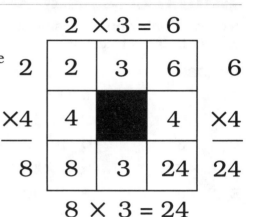

$$2 \times 3 = 6$$

$$8 \times 3 = 24$$

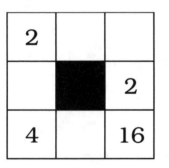

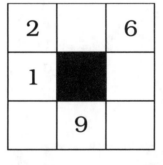

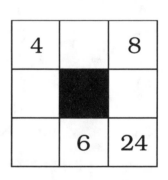

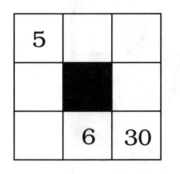

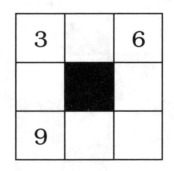

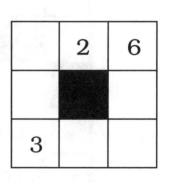

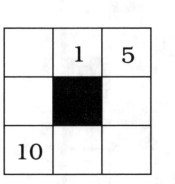

Jumbo Cross-Number Puzzle

A cross-number puzzle is similar to a crossword puzzle. Solve each problem. Write the answer in the correct boxes going across or down. Write only one digit in each box.

ACROSS

A 6×6	**N** 6×5	**A** 8×4	**M** 10×2
B 4×4	**P** 5×10	**B** 2×6	**N** 5×6
C 7×3	**Q** 10×6	**C** 7×4	**O** 7×10
D 6×7	**R** 1×10	**D** 7×7	**P** 5×10
E 3×6	**S** 4×10	**E** 2×5	**Q** 10×6
G 9×11	**T** 7×10	**F** 7×5	**R** 2×8
H 10×5	**U** 9×4	**G** 10×9	**S** 5×9
I 5×5	**V** 3×4	**H** 5×10	**T** 8×9
J 8×5	**W** 4×5	**I** 8×3	**U** 10×3
K 6×10	**Y** 9×5	**J** 6×8	**V** 5×3
L 2×7	**Z** 10×7	**K** 8×8	**W** 5×4
M 6×4	**ZZ** 4×9	**L** 10×1	**X** 6×6

DOWN

Window-Frame Multiplication

By now, your students have learned the multiplication tables for the 0's through 9s, and they've even done their 10s.

What happens next? Students should now be ready to multiply larger two-digit numbers. Of course, the strategy for this still depends on knowing the one-digit tables.

For example:

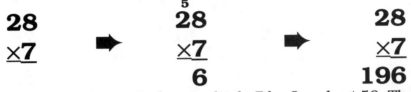

To find the answer, students usually first multiply 7 by 8 and get 56. They write the 6 under the 7, and carry the 5.

Next, they multiply 7 by 2 and get 14. After adding the 5 that was carried over, they get 19. This is the traditional way of solving higher multiplication. However, you can also use "window-frame multiplication" for solving problems with two and more digits. It's a different approach that your students might find interesting. Here's how it works:

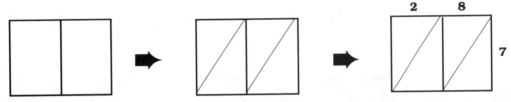

Students begin by drawing a window frame for each digit being multiplied in the top line. In the example above, the number 28 has two digits, so you draw two windows.

The number on the second line (7) has only one digit, so the design is made only one frame deep.

Next, each window frame is divided with a diagonal line. The numbers to be multiplied are written above and to the right of the window frames. Starting from the right, first multiply 7 by 8. The answer is recorded in the right window.

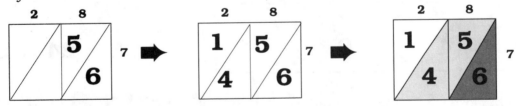

Next, multiply 7 by 2. The answer is written in the left window. Notice the three diagonal areas. Look at the numbers in each area. If there are two numbers in a diagonal area, add them together (for example, 4 + 5 = 9) . Finally, starting from the left, read the numbers across—1, then 9, then 6. Your answer is 196!

$$28 \times 7 = 196$$

Window-frame multiplication can be used with any number of digits. For example:

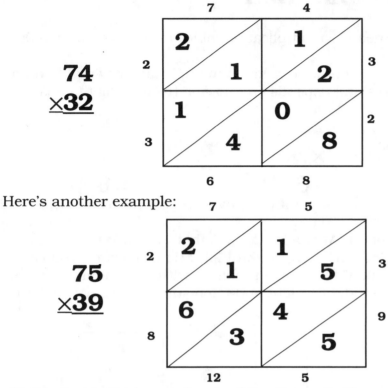

74
×32

74 × 32 = 2,368

Here's another example:

75
×39

75 × 39 = 2,925

Notice that in this example one of the diagonal columns adds up to a two-digit number—in this case, 12. When this happens, you simply add the tens digit of this number (1) to the number to its left (8). Thus, 2-8-12-5 becomes 2-9-2-5.

Window-frame multiplication can be used for three-digit numbers, too:

603
×24

603 × 24 = 14,472

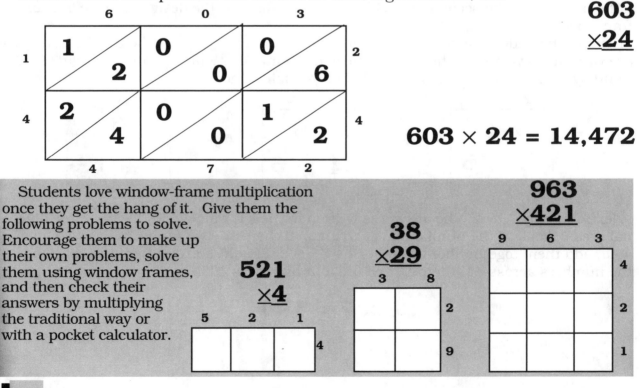

Students love window-frame multiplication once they get the hang of it. Give them the following problems to solve. Encourage them to make up their own problems, solve them using window frames, and then check their answers by multiplying the traditional way or with a pocket calculator.

521
×4

38
×29

963
×421

Games for the Classroom

Nothing reinforces multiplication skills like a fun-filled game! The following pages offer several suggestions for classroom players.

Buzz

This game helps review multiples of a specific number. It can be played with the entire class or in small groups.

The leader chooses a number between 2 and 9, such as 6, and announces it to the class. The leader then counts "1"; the student to his left counts "2"; the next student counts "3"; and so on. When the counting reaches a multiple of 6, the counter for that number must call out "Buzz!" instead of a number.

With the number 6, counting would go like this:

One...two...three...four...five...BUZZ...seven...eight...nine...ten...eleven...BUZZ... and so on.

If a player forgets to say "BUZZ!" at the proper time or says it at the wrong time, other players in the group may correct him.

Continue the counting until the last number of multiples through 9 has been reached. (In the case of 6, the last number would be 54.)

Begin a new round using a new number.

• **VARIATION 1:** Players call out "Buzz!" for any number that is a multiple of or merely contains the digit. For example, with the number 4, counting would go: "1, 2, 3, BUZZ, 5, 6, 7, BUZZ, 9, 10, 11, BUZZ, 13, BUZZ, 15, BUZZ..." and so on.

• **VARIATION 2:** Players play with two different numbers simultaneously, such as 3 and 5. On a multiple of 3, they say "Buzz." On a multiple of 5, they say "Fizz." On a multiple of both 3 and 5, they say "Buzz-Fizz." For example: "1, 2, BUZZ, 4, FIZZ, BUZZ, 7, 8, BUZZ, FIZZ, 11, BUZZ, 13, 14, BUZZ-FIZZ..." and so on.

Multiplication Card Game

Here's a game for two students to play with a deck of cards. Remove the jokers and picture cards. Have students shuffle the deck and each take half. Tell them to keep their cards facedown in a pile. Distribute the reproducible Times Table (on page 45) for them to check their answers against.

To start the game, each player flips over the top card from her pile so her opponent can see it. The first player to call out the correct product of the two numbers gets to keep both cards, which are set aside in a separate pile next to the player. If a player calls out an incorrect product, both cards go to the opponent.

Players continue to flip over their cards and follow the same procedure as before, until all their cards have been played. Then they each shuffle the cards they have accumulated and begin a second round of play.

The object of the game is to accumulate all the cards. The player who eventually does so is the winner.

Around-the-Solar-System Game

This game is for two, three, or four players. Distribute one copy of the game board on page 59 to each group. The group also needs two sets of index cards, each set having the numbers 1 through 9 on it (one number per card).

At the start of the game, players put their markers on the START squares. All 18 cards are shuffled.

Player A picks any two cards at random, multiplies the number, and announces the product. If his answer is correct and the product appears on the first planet (Mercury), player A places his marker on the planet. If his answer is wrong or his product does not appear on the planet, he stays where he is. The two cards are put back anywhere in the pile, and player B then pulls two cards at random. He follows the same procedure as before.

Each time a player finds his product on the planet, he may move his marker there. The first player to reach the ninth planet (Pluto) wins the game.

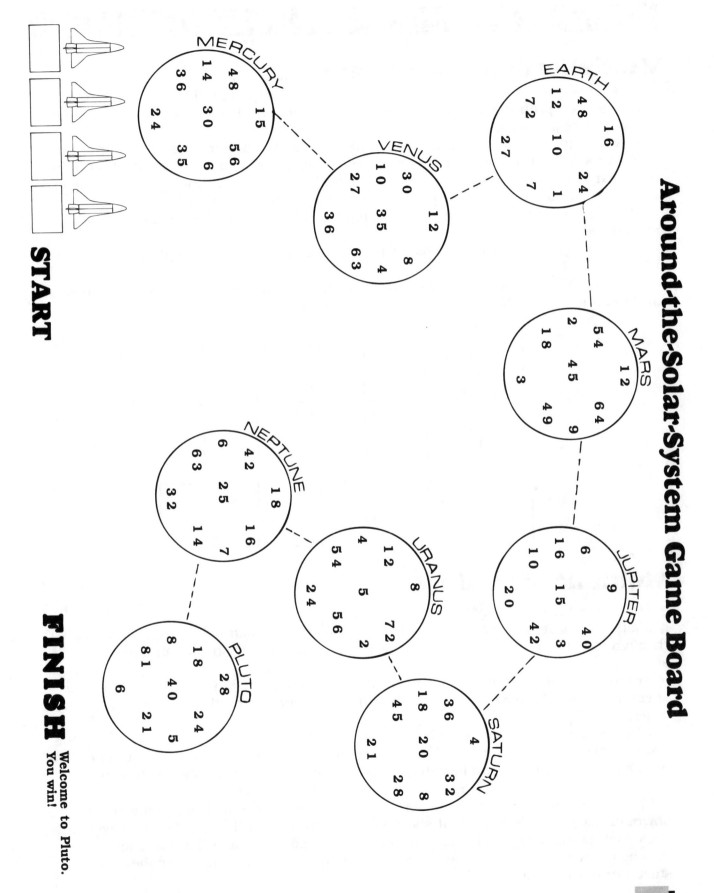

Around-the-Solar-System Game Board

START

MERCURY
15
48
14 30
36
24 35 6

VENUS
30
10 35
27
36 63 4 8
12

EARTH
16
48 24
12 10 1
72 7
27

MARS
12
54 64
2 45 9
18 49
3

JUPITER
9
6 40
16 15 3
10 42
20

SATURN
4
36 32
18 20 8
45 28
21

URANUS
8
12 72
4 5 2
54 56
24

NEPTUNE
18
42 16
6 25 7
63 14
32

PLUTO
28
18 24
8 40 5
81 21
6

FINISH Welcome to Pluto. You win!

XXXXXXXXXXXXXXXXXXXXXXXXX

Multiplication Concentration

This game is designed for two or three players. To prepare, write twelve different multiplication problems on index cards, one per card. On twelve other cards, write the answers, one per card.

Players shuffle all 24 cards and place them facedown in four rows of six cards each.

Player A turns over two cards. If one card shows a problem (such as 8 × 4) and the other card shows its product (in this case 32), the player keeps those cards. If the two cards do not match, they are turned facedown again in their rows.

Player B then flips two more cards, trying to find the match, and following the same procedure.

The game continues until all 24 cards have been collected by the players. The player with the most cards wins.

VARIATION: You may play with a different number of cards (such as ten problems and ten answers, or 18 problems and 18 answers).

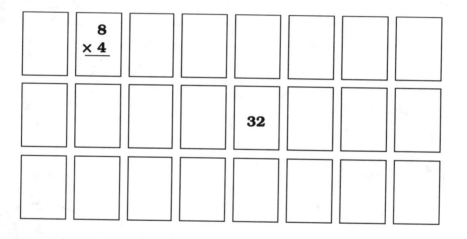

Multiplication Bingo

The entire class can play this game at once.

Make a separate index card for each multiplication problem involving numbers 0 through 9. Duplicate the bingo card on the following page. Distribute one to each student.

Instruct the children to choose any 25 of the numbers shown at the bottom of their sheet, and have them write each number in its own square on the bingo sheet, in any order.

When students are done, shuffle your problem cards and pick the top card. Say the problem aloud. (For example: "Five times three.") Any student with the product of that problem (in this case 15) on her bingo sheet should cover the number with a small marker.

Continue calling problems until someone has covered five numbers going across, down, or diagonally. The student should call "Multiplication Bingo!" As the player calls back each product to you, make sure you have called a problem that matches it. Play as many winners per game as you like before having children clear their cards to start a brand-new game.

Name: _____

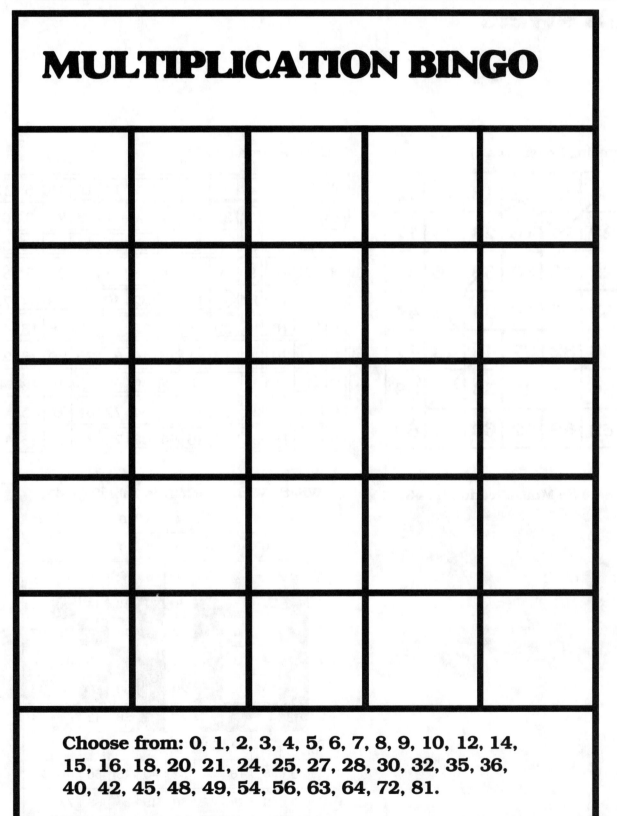

MULTIPLICATION BINGO

Choose from: 0, 1, 2, 3, 4, 5, 6, 7, 8, 9, 10, 12, 14, 15, 16, 18, 20, 21, 24, 25, 27, 28, 30, 32, 35, 36, 40, 42, 45, 48, 49, 54, 56, 63, 64, 72, 81.

Answers

Break the Code (p. 20)

in the forest

Five Fill-in (p. 22)

V

'Mazing Seven (p. 28)

7	6	21	16	9	15
20	14	16	28	25	12
29	26	30	35	36	31
38	22	40	39	42	44
46	32	37	49	43	47
50	54	45	53	56	59
62	68	52	60	65	63

Pattern Search (p. 37)

4	8	2	4	6	8	10	12	14	16	18	5	12
1	9	12	3	32	72	6	7	8	18	21	8	63
2	10	9	6	4	8	12	16	20	24	28	32	36
3	7	16	9	40	49	18	28	21	30	35	9	81
4	32	12	12	8	16	24	32	40	48	56	64	72
5	5	10	15	20	25	30	35	40	45	48	18	40
6	24	20	18	49	81	36	40	81	35	20	28	21
7	7	14	21	28	35	42	49	56	63	9	42	4
8	18	16	24	63	21	48	64	72	64	6	35	2
9	9	18	27	36	45	54	63	72	81	2	16	18

Real-Life Multiplication (p. 43)

1. 45
2. 27
3. 36
4. 16

Special Challenge:

5 hot dog packages;
4 bun packages

What's Wrong with This Table? (p. 47)

×	0	1	2	3	4	5	6	7	8	9
0	0	0	0	0	0	0	0	0	0	0
1	0	1	2	3	4	5	6	7	8	9
2					8		12	14		18
3		3	6		12		18		24	27
4		4	8		16			28	32	36
5		5	10		20		30		40	45
6					24		36	42		54
7	0	7	14	21	28	35	42	49	56	63
8	0	8	16	24	32	40	48	56	64	72
9	0	9	18	27	36	45	54	63	72	81

Problem Hunt (p. 48)

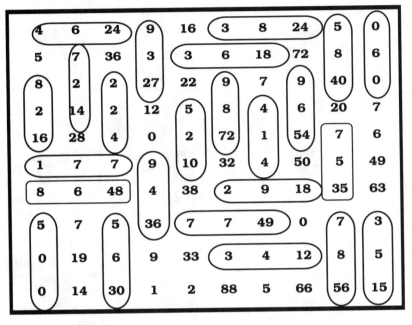

The Same But Different (p. 49)

MULTIPLIER

The Secret Message (p. 50)

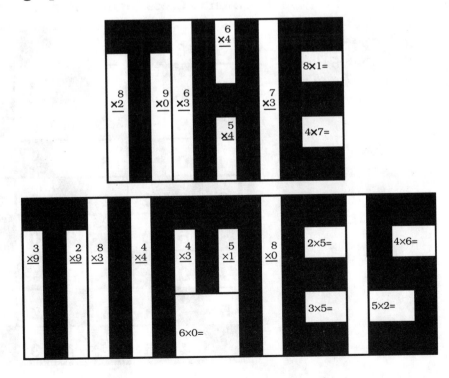

Whats Dot? (p. 51)

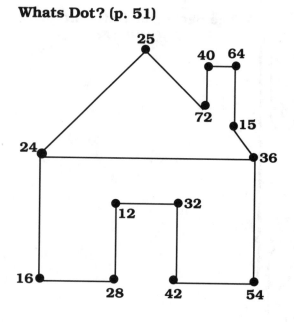

Magic Squares (p. 53)

2	4	8
2	■	2
4	4	16

2	3	6
1	■	3
2	9	18

4	2	8
1	■	3
4	6	24

5	1	5
1	■	6
5	6	30

3	2	6
3	■	3
9	2	18

3	2	6
1	■	4
3	8	24

5	1	5
2	■	4
10	2	20

2	2	4
5	■	5
10	2	20

7	4	28
9	■	0
63	0	0

Number Jumbles (p. 52)

4×7=28; 5×5=25; 3×6=18;
2×9=18; 4×5=20; 8×8=64;
7×9=63; 3×9=27; 6×9=54;
7×7=49; 6×7=42;

Jumbo Cross-Number Puzzle (p. 54)

A 3	6	■	B 1	6	■	C 2	1	■
2	■	D 4	2	■	E 1	8	■	F 3
■	G 9	9	■	H 5	0	■	I 2	5
J 4	0	■	K 6	0	■	L 1	4	■
8	■	M 2	4	■	N 3	0	■	O 8
■	P 5	0	■	Q 6	0	■	R 1	0
S 4	0	■	T 7	0	■	U 3	6	■
5	■	V 1	2	■	W 2	0	■	X 3
■	Y 4	5	■	Z 7	0	■	ZZ 3	6